While every prec̶a̶u̶t̶i̶o̶n̶ ̶h̶a̶s̶ ̶b̶e̶e̶n̶ ̶t̶a̶k̶e̶n̶ ̶i̶n̶ ̶t̶h̶e̶ ̶p̶r̶e̶p̶a̶r̶a̶t̶i̶o̶n̶ of this book, the publisher assumes no responsibility for errors or omissions, or for damages resulting from the use of the information contained herein.

PELOSI'S PLEDGE

First edition. February 15, 2021.

Copyright © 2021 Phil Berto.

Written by Phil Berto.

DEDICATION

"We have to pass it to see what's in it." – Nancy Pelosi
"You re-elected her. Dumbass." – Phil Berto

Gillibrand (Who?) Glossary
Republic: shared responsibility and accountability; all con-
tribute <u>something</u>.
Democracy: mob rule; welfare run amok; a nation of parasites;
all get free phones.

Also by Phil Berto:
SNIPPETS – COMMENTS FROM THE RED
SNIPPED – AMERICA POST #ME TOO
SNIPS – COMMENTS FROM THE BLACK AND BLUE
SNAPPED – COMMENTS FROM A C-C-CONSERVA-
TIVE
SNAPPER – THE LIBERAL FINGER
UNSNAPPED – OBEDIENT LIB-RAL EDITION
FIVE SLEAZY SLIPPETS AND A MISSIVE OR TWO

PREFACE

THE LIMITS OF SHORT TERM
The richest country in South America is now a hell-hole. Advantage: progressives.

For ~~men~~ persons* who supposedly think on a planetary level, globalists fail to see the Big Picture. Killing the middle class by, say, opening the borders and purging pipelines may garner cheaper labor and higher fuel prices (Thank you, environmentalist know-nothings/witless tools of corporatists), but there will be no one left to buy your products. Hot Tip: Visit Venezuela. Dumbass.

*You are N.O.W. required to pretend that some of these assholes are women.

Editrix: Russia is struggling. China can't feed its overpopulation. Europe is... Europe*. They hated seeing U.S. so successful. Thanks to Obiden and the ninnies who Found A Way to deflect their desire to support a family of on-the-take 47-year political hacks, they no longer have to. Misery loves company, and our liberal establishment just gave it to them. Dumbass.

*The **Gillibrand (Who?) Glossary** defines this. "Europe": fucked up.

4

FIREFIGHTERS WHO VOTED AS TOLD BY THE UNION:

Check out your pension fund performance next year. Dumbass.

N O NEWS IS FOX NEWS
New Fox News mentioned D-D-Dominion last night!

Q: what did NFN say about D-D-Dominion?

A: Nothin'.

Q: So why did NFN bother to <u>mention</u> D-D-Dominion?

A: So we can't say they never mention it, Silly.

SEE? WE AIRED THE STORY. DO WE GET A COOKIE?

To comply with COVID constrictions, an LA restauranteur built a tent café outside her brick-and-mortar. To feed its film crew, a movie company set up the same shit across the street. Guess which one got shut down.

The movie moguls would have spent less, and saved a small business in the bargain, had they simply leased the <u>already there</u> concern a few steps away from where they put their canteen; so why didn't they? Do they know the mayor, politically or biblically? Did they fund his campaign? Did they get a pass just for being lib-ral? Maybe someone on the New Fox No News will "push them a bit", unless, of course, they're owned by D-D-Dominion or some other Chinese Communist enterprise. Anyway, they aired just enough of the story to (barely) keep their conservative creds, so expect no follow-up.

- For Angela Marsden, Pineapple Saloon & Grill, Los Angeles

~~SOURCES~~ RELIABLE SOURCES SAY...

"So, aren't ballots <u>always</u> kept in suitcases?"

Q: If an anonymous anti-Trump whistleblower is a hero to CNN, what is a poll worker who stands up in court under oath?

A: Ignored.

THE ANTI-ESTABLISHMENT ESTABLISHMENT

Then: The left is anti-war, anti-big gov-mint, anti-big banks.

Now. The left pickd a 47-year political hack over a populist DC outsider who is anti-war, anti-big gov-mint, anti-big banks.

Q: Is this irony?

A: Stupidity.

Q: Don't that make them the useful idiots of Marx & Engels?

A: DontcarehateTrump.

Att lib-rals: If you think cherry-picking whistleblowers to bolster your bias is cool, you're <u>really</u> gonna like:

WEIRD SCIENCE ACCORDING TO CNN

1-A corporate conglomerate outlet packed with people cannot COVID spread.

2-A mom & pop restaurant at 25% capacity will fucking kill you.

Q: Gee, d'ya think Obiden's buddies in Big Tech/Media/Banks are corporatists?

A: DontcarehateTrump.

SO WHAT ELSE IS GNU?

Tired of the Serengeti Special, the senior lion spotted a yuppiewithwhistle. Yum.

GALA GRATUITOUS VIOLENCE SECTION

JUKE JOINT
Problem: The jerk won't quite give you cause to slug him.
Solution: Say, "I don't want no trouble". Emboldened by your sniveling, <u>he will come at you</u>. Problem solved.

OUT-WEAPONED BUT NOT OUT-ARMED by Kenfo Llett-Berto

Like all farriers through the ages, he was as likely as not to have a hammer in hand, if not tongs. Thus he greeted the Welsh nobleman's son, who brought in a courser which had thrown a shoe. Thus he bade him farewell, still awaiting payment for an expert repair that included a lift to correct what his practiced eye had noted as a labored gait.

"I am soon to be a knight", puffed the young pretender. "When I inherit, I will own this squalid hamlet. You should be honored to do me this service."

When the smith's son stepped up to protest, Sir Almost-Knight spun his mount into him, sending the lad sprawling with a thud. Mr. Smith had seen men trampled at Agincourt, sharpened stakes notwithstanding. By pure reflex, he brought his hammer down on the horse's forehead. As the stunned animal crumpled, his owner drew his sword, screaming, "I'll cut you to pieces!". The hammer fell again, shattering the welsher's kneecap. Moving like a leopard, Smith pulled the punk from the now-lowered saddle, relieved him of his dagger, and thrust it into the horse's heart to end its kicking (and its suffering; the man's profession had fostered a fondness for his charges).

"My father will have you hanged", sobbed the near-knight. Smith now turned the dirk on him. "You will be the first one-eyed bastard ever to keep vigil", he breathed, doubly enraged at the sheer needlessness us of the event. "Your father and I go way back. You are his least-favorite son. He will believe my account of this: you were thrown and your horse ran off. My wagoner carted you to the surgeon in exchange for your sword. No matter how many men you muster, if you return you will be the first to die. One more word will be your last. Tell His Lordship to expect a cask of salt horse on the fortnight with my compliments."

Note: Do you want to know a secret? Young snotty lived to marry and breed. His knightly wish was granted to his progeny generations later by the desperate act of a dying empire. The feat? "We all live in a yellow submarine." Promise not to tell. Do-da-do.

A NATION OF PRETENDERS NO MORE

Two generations ago we began consulting professional pretenders for socio-political guidance. We actually listened when a ninny like DeNiro extolled the virtue of Cuomo's killing of 5,000 seniors for nothing more than political correctness. Now the actor wants to punch the President in the face. Bob. Asshole. The real world has no script. People out here will punch you back. So pretend all day long in front of a movie camera, then shut the fuck up. The Biden "election" hoax has awakened U.S. Your words off-set are meaningless.

SMARMY

1. What your ass feels like when you wipe when you should have washed.

2. Bill Mahr.

NEVER GO AGAINST THE OBIDEN FAMILY BUSINESS AGAIN. – Don Vito Corleone-Berto

Faux News 12/11/20 @ 2230 hours: This just in...

"The Supreme Court has refused to hear the Texas case challenging the "election" of biden/HARRIS. We now return to the Pablum Angle."

Note: The United States of America just became a vassal of Communist China, and New Fox No News went back to the gay Grinch & Friends. It's <u>over</u>.

Q: The election?

A: The Western civilization.

I ONLY BUY IT FOR THE ARTICLES. – Mierda DeToro

"What kind of man reads Playboy?" Thus began an ad that ran in every issue. (I would know.) How sexist! "Man". "Play<u>boy</u>". We don't do that 'round here; we are awakened. To offer the chicks separate-but-equal time, we give you:

"What sort of broad voted Obiden?" We begin with the original, a troll who donned a North Vietnamese Army Helmet, ~~manned~~ personned a North Vietnamese anti-aircraft gun, and pretended to shoot down the fathers, husbands, brothers and sons of her ~~countrymen~~ countrypersons. Her likeness still appears on urinal cakes in VFW halls throughout the land, even though I think she might be dead. Let us not forget the mothers, wives, sisters and daughters who bought Barbarella's workout video. Note: This degree of disloyalty was not lost on North Vietnam's sponsor, The People's Redundant Democratic Republic of Communist Fucking China. Within one generation they had the entire Biden Family (and U.S.) by the balls. Benedict Swalwell was child's play for them.

"Everyone who has seen That Face knows she is Mephistopheles", but where'd Witmer find her evil twin, the deaf & dumb language signer? These two scaries <u>wake up</u> pissed off. Governor Gretchen defended Beelzebub, who had taken the form of Cynthia Johnson* when Ms. Thing called Trumpers "haters" and exhorted lib-rals to lynch them because they are "divisive".

*Looked better as himself.

ps: Gretchen's husband, the bravest/dumbest man on Earth (What was he thinking?) named his boat the Edmund Fitzgerald II. Big II carries a dinghy/tender named, "Death Wish". Look it up.

WASTE NOT YE FOOD – St. Paul-Berto

"Half my money went to fast women; the other half got wasted."

I'll stuff $5 bills into a "dancer's" shoes all night long, but I hate finding a hot dog/science project in the back of the refrigerator.

TWO-WAY TOADIES

"This will not be a second Obama Administration." It will be the first Jake Tapper administration.

CATS VS KIDS

Cats eat, sleep, wreck the furniture, love you to death, get fixed for $50.

Kids eat, sleep, wreck the furniture, hate your guts, get knocked-up.

TARDY

En route to the tattoo parlor, Mother changed her mind at the last possible instant.

Q: No tatt?

A: No baby.

PEOPLE GET THE MOB RULE THEY DESERVE. – Voltaire-Berto

Like every enslaved nation, we let our news become propaganda, our information become censored, our leaders become whores to the highest biden, I mean, bidder.

The globalists are correct: the world will be better as China takes U.S. over. True, we don't kill as many viable babies, but our methods are the same, and lib-rals have Found A Way to see that we all have a hand in it by using our taxes to fund abortion mills/ baby body parts emporia like PPH.

China is going to inherit a lotta healthy hussies, what with all those WHIs. This may help Chinese women, who are sickly by comparison, since they have no WHIs. The poor dears still call LTA and PBA what they are: infanticide. Maybe N.O.W. they'll wise up, commit more WHIs, and get healthy again.

Gillibrand* Glossary
PPH: Planned Parent Hood.
WHI: Women's "Health" Issues.
LTA: Infanticide
PBA: Infanticide
*Q: Is Kirsten dead?
A: Who cares?

THERE WILL BE NO SECOND LATTE

Pickin' up chicks in Starbucks is tough. Her hero was Che Guevarra. My hero was, and is, the man who shot the son of a bitch.

FOR FUNDAMENTAL INACCURACIES OF BIBLICAL PROPORTIONS, ASK ANY MINISTER

You wrote a tech manual for a state-of-the-art computerized weapon system. In Aramaic and Hebrew. It was translated into Greek, then Latin, then ancient English, then Olde English which, thou wilt recall, was the modern English* of the day. Now act surprised when the dam-ned contrivance doth wrought fire and brimstone on the wrong-ed people.

Moral: Ye annum II study in tax exemption yon biblical scholar maketh not.

*Be ye saying that God doth not really speaketh that way? How odd.

NOW WE KNOW <u>WHAT</u> REPRESENTATIVE CYNTHIA JOHNSON REPRESENTS

Why are we surprised when these devils call for killing cops, conservatives and freedom? They kill their own offspring via the most brutal methods imaginable, long after baby can feel pain and <u>cry</u>. Right about now, feminists are covering their ears, holding their breath and stamping their feet, but if you did this shit to a puppy you would be arrested. Hear me roar.

NOT ANY MORE

"We are not just an economy in some global marketplace. We are a Nation with a cultural reason for being." – Steve Bannon

"Past tense." – P. Berto

FOX NEWS WAS ALL OVER the Smartmatic/Dominion story, but then (pay attention) <u>Joe tripped over his dog</u>.

WHAT KIND OF MAN (BUN) ~~READS PLAYBOY~~ VOTES BIDEN

So, begins every utterance with, "so"?

So, ends every inanity with "?"?

So, texts someone who is in the same room?

So, texts while driving?

So, <u>drives while texting</u>?

So, puts 50¢ candy bar on his/her/undecided's Visa/EBT card?

So, holds up the line at lunch time to get $20 back?

So, hugs tree, wipes spills with Bounty?

So, hates water bottles, recycles nothing?

So, hugs tree, throws out boxes when moving from Beemer to loft?

So, must have designer washer/dryer, makes payments on-nit?

So, puts designer washer/dryer on second floor?

So, never knew designer washer/dryer could throw a hose?

So, wonders why ceiling falls, first floor floods?

So, readers are invited to make up their own JoeKammys (jokes-a-mes)?

SAVING THE PLANET, ONE DUMBASS AT A TIME

woman: a being, some say sentient, who...

– drags out a motorized contraption (But it's cordless!) to pick up a handful of whatever 'cause she don't own no b-b-broom.* Said contrivance must then be cleaned/emptied/charged/etc.

– pays double for drawstring garbage bags because she is incapable of changing a cheap dog-eared bag before it is too full to tie.

– buys a "sustainable" forest product called Bounty to save rinsing out a rag. Hot Tip: the sink has running water, and it's <u>right there</u>. You don't have to take it down to the creek and beat it on a rock.

Sustainable: yuppiespeak for: you can re-plant it. Okay, some trees are grown for pulpwood. So far, so good. Enter fossil fuel-burning trucks & equipment to harvest them. Still not so bad, and it employs good working folks. Now think about how harsh the chemical needs to be to break wood down into cellulose fibers. Gee, maybe that's why you can smell the paper mill 20 miles away. Dumbass.

*There are, of course, exceptions. My ex had a broom. It's how she got around.

MISSION STATEMENT: OUR HAND IS ALWAYS OUT, AND IT AIN'T FOR "WELCOME".

With a Biden presidency looming, the State Department rushed to gush about "the return of diplomacy". Yay.

Diplomacy (Department of State): actively seek ways to put foreign interests above ours, without a care as to the cost in American lives, jobs & treasure. A Secretary of State might even arrange a transfer of fucking uranium to, say, Russia (China had enough) and then say Trump colluded. See: seat of disloyalty.

ps: U.S. is down a buncha U-235, Clinton foundation is up $1 zillion. Do-dah.

ps: CNN-DNC, NBC-DNC MSNBC-DNC, NYT-DNC, WAPO-DNC: not a peep.

Fox News: dropped it when the real story broke: Joe tripped over his dog.

CRAVEN COVID CABAL

Close to restaurants. Open the borders. (I guess all the invaders have been tested.)

REALITY CHECKMATE

First cold snap. Crack a window. 2 blankets + 2 cats (didn't have 2 dogs). Slept like a baby. Real oatmeal and venison sausage for breakfast. Short drive to CVS for the meds that keep me alive. Ran into a guy I usta ride with. Regional Champion. Heard he's still real fast. We reminisced a bit, and I almost felt young. Then. He. Said. It. "Is that your golf cart?" Thanks, Borge.

OH MY GOD, I AM HARDLY SORRY...

Been roundly (and squarely) criticized for assigning an Italian accent to a Pope who Hail Marys from Argentina. Allow me to make restitution*.

Q: Yo, Pope. What's your fav Popemobile?

A: Bibdy-seben Cheby wee stannaad tdans-mee-shown.

*To cover theft traced to invaders they harbor in NHETA neighborhoods, Catholic Services now makes restitution... <u>Kidding</u>!

NHETA: Not His Excellency The Archbishop's.

PAVE THE PLANET

Have a cat? Get sawdust. It's free at any lumber mill/truss factory/cabinet shop. (Yuppies: you <u>could</u> kick in a couple bucks for their coffee kitty, but you won't.) Sawdust bulks-up cat litter, which is expensive, and picks up cat puke, which is not. Ladies may disregard: you drag out the Dyson for the smallest dry bills and throw a buncha Bounty on the largest wet ones 'counta you don't own a b-b-broom and won't r-r-rinse out a r-r-rag. Hug a tree.

Editrix: Bro. You need to back off. The poor dear buys egg -shaped Tupperware because peeling an egg confuses her. Cut her some hear me roar slack.

THE RIGHT ENEMIES

"Trump is hated by the leaders of foreign countries." – any lib-ral.

Bingo! Dumbass. They hate his guts because he nixxed their lopsided trade deals and got U.S. out of useless sops to weird science like the Paris Accord, which U.S. (of course) would have funded to cripple our own economy while all the heavy polluters got a 10-year pass. Gee, d'ya think that 10 years down the line they will renege and take their 10-year jump on U.S. to the bank? Dumbass.

Greece hates that Trump won't let U.S. cover their fiscal irresponsibility. NATO countries hate that Trump makes them pay their fair share. Iran hates that Trump won't let U.S. send them pallets of Obama/Biden/Kerry "Please don't hurt U.S.," cash. Oh my! We might have to use our awesome military to defend U.S. instead of squandering our blood and treasure on "nationbuilding". The horror!

Q: Remember when lib-rals thought that staying out of war was a Good Thing?

A: DontcarehateTrump.

FOX ON FOX

"See? I was right! I was right!"

Yay. We still just lost our Country.

WHAT TRUMP DID WRONG

Called a fat chick "Miss Piggy". Everybody knows it is N.O.W. "Ms. Piggy".

TRUMP 4 YEARS	OBIDEN 8 YEARS
VA reform (fired 9,000)	Nope.
Otto Warmbier home	Nope.
Prison sentence reform	Nope.
Cancel Iran deal	Made Iran deal.
Nix Paris accord	Sucked into Paris Accord.
Pardoned over-sentenced Blacks	Say, what?
Coal miners resume work	Gov-mint regs killed coal.
Pipeline approved	Pipeline stopped.
Fracking fine	Fracking bad.
USA energy independent	USA at mercy of Arabs.
US Embassy moved to Jerusalem	Promise broken for 30 years.
$50,000 existing building versus $2,000,000 to build new (gov-mint wet dream)	Huh?
Israel controls Golan Heights	Waa?
Treaty: Israel + 3 Arab States	Eeh?
Close borders	Close restaurants, open borders.
Stop China travel	Racist! Xenophobic!
10,000 – 30,000 per rally	10 – 30 per rally (blow horns!)
Nope	3 strikes law targets Blacks.
Sent Sting missiles to help Ukraine Fight Russia.	Sent blankets & MREs.
Nope	Withheld $6,000,000 in defense aid 'till Hunter investigation stopped.

TRUMP 4 YEARS	OBIDEN 8 YEARS
Nope	School integration "creates a racial jungle."
Nope	China pays son $5 million.
Nope	Burisma pays son $50,000/month.
Celebrates American exceptionalism	Denies American exceptionalism.
Killed MS–13	¿Que?

STATISTICALLY IMPOSSIBLE REAL WORLD FRAUD	LIB-RAL LAND BUTTERFLIES & RAINBOWS
Hide in cellar, get most votes ever	Isn't that wonderful?
Can barely speak, more votes than Hillary	Isn't that wonderful?
Racist past, more black votes than Obama	Isn't that wonderful?
Dominion voting machines from China	Isn't that wonderful?
Pelosi/Feinstein spouse on Dominion board	What's your point?
Late votes had postmark changed	How nice!
5000 Army votes dumped, all Biden	See? Soldiers like Joe!
Votes without signatures counted	Maybe they forgot.
TELL ME WHAT TRUMP DID WRONG	TELL ME WHAT BIDEN DID RIGHT

IRONY

Blacks vote for the Party of segregation; now they choose all-talk Biden over all-action Trump.

"RESISTANCE": RIOT TO MAINTAIN STATUS QUO (SEE: UNWITTING CORPORATIST TOOL)

Ho Lee Fuk: One round-eye aircraft carrier can poof Peking. How we beat U.S.?

No Tso Dum: 47-year poritical hack sell out Country, do our bidening.

HLF: He need take out populist president. How he do that?

NTD: So easy. Yutes support big banks, big Pharma, big tech, big media.

HLF: Why they do that?

NTD: We tell them they "resistance". Say everyting so backwards. They accept.

HLF: Why they so dumb?

NTD: Again, 3 generations pot smoke parent/friends, libral teacher-indoctrinator.

HLF: Rib-rals say conservatives backwards.

NTD: Rib-rals see Russia, Cuba, Venezuela, say "Let's try here". Who backwards?

HLF: That backwards?

NTD: That nuts.

HLF: Why pretty lady Fox NoNews not say "resistance" is opposite?

NTD: Pretty lady like waggle jewelry, say Joe trip on dog, break foot (so sad).

HLF: Maybe earring fall off so something happen on her show.

NTD: That not scare Chinaman. Ha, ha!

HLF: What kind parent preach pot smoke?

NTD: Ask Lob Dyldek on Ledicurousness.

HLF: Steelo Brim say white kid on small boat "priveleged". Kid racist?

NTD: Everybody on boat racist 'till everybody have boat. see: reparations.

HLF: Country sounds frucked up. Maybe we should give back.

NIB: Maybe Joe eat dog name Smartmatic/Dominion. Pretty lady drop earring. Ha-ha.

EYES WIDE OPEN

"I'm worth more to you alive than dead." -Ernesto "Che" Guevarra

"Te puedes comer un tambo de mierda." -(Pa-chow!) -ciudadano-soldado de Bolivia

My favorite fotografia of starry-eyed Che shows him on a slab with a bullet hole in his black heart. Att tie-dye, macrame', Birkenstock kumbaya crowd: I'd wear <u>that</u> T-shirt. Peace.

GALLAGHER FODDER

They literally lack the ability to sharpen a knife. To chop an onion, dice a potato, slice a tomato, etc., they deploy a motorized, computer-controlled contraption that takes longer to clean than the meal takes to eat. No wonder bitch pays quadruple for grub hub.

Q: Are these the same yuppie broads who drag out a Dyson for a small spill because a b-b-broom baffles them?

A: Bro. Peeling an egg confuses them; hence egg-shaped tupperware. Hear me roar.

COVID'S COSTING THEM MONEY, SO THE BISHOPS
ARE SPEAKING OUT FOR OPENING UP.

Q: Are these the same prelates who preach about leaving
Christmas decorations up until the Epiphany (Hell's Bells,
Padre; I'm sick of them by Thanksgiving) but won't say a syllable
about late-term/partial-birth infanticide?

A: Like I said, covid's costing 'em money. Pissing off their
progressive parishioners is the last thing they want to do. Amen.

THE STATE DEPARTMENT

Celebrates the "return of diplomacy" Biden will bring.
Translation: US. pays the tab.

LIB-RAL LOGIC CIRCLES THE BOWL

TRUMP BAD	BIDEN GOOD
They say Trump lied 2,347 times.	Trump does bad things.
Q: About what?	Q: Like what?
A: Wassa difference?	A: Things.
Q: Who are "they"?	Q: What does Biden do?
A: Don't know.	A: Good things.
Q: Anonymous?	Q: Like what?
A: Dontcarehatetrump.	A: Dontcarehatetrump.

LIB-RALS WILL HAND THE COUNTRY OVER TO
SOME CRUEL BASTARDS, THEN PICK PRONOUNS

Not talkin' 'bout folks who fight dogs & roosters. They won't be running things. Biden sold out to people who kill and butcher dogs in front of other (caged) dogs.

Q: Do they think dogs are not sentient beings?

A: They don't give a shit. see: cruel bastards.

When the middle class is destroyed and U.S. is just another third world hell-hole with only the very rich (globalists) and the very poor (you), just like our southern socialist neighbors (¿Que?), churches will suffer, since middle-class conservatives have always been the most generous (lib-rals just talk about it). RELAX. The Holy Spirit has ended his/her/its 2,000-year sabbatical and sent relief, straight from our now-open southern border. ¿See? The Bishop can replace bingo with blood sports to boost betting/bolster benefaction so he and his boss can keep their walled enclaves while we build bridges with boards from the hovels which the now-extinct middle class will be consigned to as voters-in-storage who must elect Democrats "to keep our shit coming".

Gillibrand (Where's ~~Hunter~~ Kirsten?) Glossary

Irony: Joe trips over dog, imports folks who fight them. Maybe Rover knows...

Karma: A fugitive harbored by Catholic Services in O.P.N.* steals the Bishop's sweet Pyrenees and sells it for use as a bait dog.

Bait dog: Know-nothing yuppies may look this up. Kumbaya, assholes.

*Other People's Neighborhoods (See also: "Prick")

Att Archbishopric: Save your absolution for yourself, priest.

ONE-TRACK MINDLESS

Congress caved to know-nothing tree huggers and stopped judicious logging

that thinned timber, then proscribed the prescribed burns that removed excess

undergrowth, resulting in heavy fuel-loading that caused the normal round of

naturally and stupidity-caused fires to defy early control. Overgrown forests

burn so hot it destroys the soil; look forward to years of slow recovery and

silted-up streams. (Yes, fire even kills fish.) Biden's answer: Appoint a

Secretary whose stated priority is to use the Department of the Interior to

combat inequality. Yay. ps: Lib-ral response: "Isn't that wonderful?"

MORE IRONY

Trump pardoned blacks who were over-sentenced by Biden policies.

Lib-ral response: "Dontcarehatetrump"

THE CHINESE DON'T MAKE MANY MISTAKES, BUT THEY SCREWED THE POOCH ON THIS ONE.

They teach math & science; the U.S.: gender-neutral pronouns. Advantage: China. All that yuan to Family Biden; China only had to <u>wait</u>.

LIB-RALS UNWITTINGLY SUPPORT RACIST IDENTI-
TY POLITICS AND <u>WANT YOU TO.</u>

Before you let racist BLM Marxists or racist Supremacists color your thinking, consider the simple words of two geniuses.

"We're all in this together." -Judge Mathis

"I didn't pick you, either." -Phil Berto

ADAM RUINS EVERY COUNTRY AS LONG AS THEY
ARE WHITE

"Rodeo is a Spanish word. If you are white and have ever rodeo'd, you should kill yourself."

Q: Don't Latinos consider themselves white?

A: Usta, 'till the hyper-race conscious left* weaponized identity politics and created the "brown" race.

*Oh, but you are the racist.

Adam's Asshole Dictionary

cultural enhancement: anything non-whites learn from whites.

cultural appropriation: anything whites steal from non-whites.

Note: If you don't think it is a compliment to adopt the best of other cultures, you might could be a lib-ral.

STOKING RACIAL HATRED 101 (NEA/AFT-AP-
PROVED COMMON CORE COURSE)

Look at their eyes. They are almost as mad as Michelle's. Today's black yutes hate their Country like their grandparents never did, and their grandparents often had reason to. Thank a teacher.

Q: Don't the presence of whites at BLM/ANTIFA riot/lootings bring the races together in perfect harmony, kumbaya?

A: Bro. when the riot/looting/vandalism is over, black thugs go back to the projects, white brats return to their parent/friends' co-ops in Manhattan and the blacks know it. So no, no it don't.

Q: But...but whites elected a black President, no?

A: No, silly, 16% of the population elected him, ail by themselves. Anyway, he goes back to his ~~roots~~ Martha's Vineyard mansion.

Gala Guest Editorial

"Vineyard, schminyard. Living with your perpetuaily-pissed off Permanent First Lady is no day at the be-otch, and it is so...so p-permanent. Thank Allah she walks the dog once in a while. There go the P-POPFIL right now."

Editrix: Holy shit. That's the P-POPFIL? I thought it was the help.

MOVE OVER, MAO

Just for Joe, Democrat machine operatives have conjured the "Office of the President-Elect", which apparently is Play Skool for fraudulently-elected... frauds. Hopefully, that will be the extent of our China Connection's "legacy", and we will get to keep our Country.

Q: WHAT DO YOU CALL a lib-ral who had a varnish brush ripped from his hand during Obiden's swat team raid (wrong wood!) on the Gibson Guitar Company?

A: A conservative.

CHRISTMAS FALLS ON A FRIDAY

Q: What's a good Pope eat?

A: Smoked Marlin. Trout. Stone crab. Lobster.

WEATHERTECH

"Behold our product. We don't know what it is, but please buy it anyway."

I know what it is not. It is not a phone. Calling it a "cup phone" will not make it so. I'd suggest "phone holder" or even "phone cup", but it would only cupfuse them. ps: Imagine what their staff meetings are like.

AS THE WORLD ROTATES

You are a lib-ral, so you cannot penetrate the difference between "Trump landslide" and "Biden fraud", so you take your Sociology Degree in Nothingness and find your old college roommate with the Master's in Statistics. He's doing tax returns for anyone who will pay him in cash (wink, wink), but he'll stop long enough to explain what "statistically impossible" means. Then you get the chick with the Psychology sheepskin to put down her "Lane Closed/Stop/Go" sign, go on break, and help you cope. Kumbaya. Peace. Butterflies & Rainbows. Planet. Coalition-Something/Something-Green. Earth. Honey Bees & Birkenstocks. Sea salt.

FORWARD TO THE PAST

For 5,600 years "scientists" told us that the Sun revolved around the Earth, which was, of course, flat. Now (get this) they say that lockdowns kill virus, so lock yourself in a fug with a family of flu spreaders. Oh, and close the windows. As usual, the opposite of what Fauci is foisting is true.

Q: What's a lib-ral <u>do</u> when gov-mint says, "Lock yourself up and don't breathe"?

A: Obey.

Q: How 'bout some fresh air & sunshine, say, on a beach?

A: Gavin closed the beaches. Opened the border, though.*

Q: What did Fauci's great, great, great, great, great, great, great, great grandfather say to Galileo?

A: "There is no such thing as a telescope, son. Follow the science."

Q: Who would do a better job than Fauci?

A: Any weasel.

*1 guess all them Mex-kins bean tested.

OOPS! THEY ~~OVERDRANK~~ ~~OVERSMOKED~~ OVERTREASONED

As ~~usual~~ always, the zeal of the left is unaccompanied by common sense. What worked with Russian peasants will not work with U.S. As dumbed-down as we have become thanks to 3 generations of pothead parent/friends and lib-ral NEA/AFT (union, no competency testing) teacher-indoctrinators, we still have some sense of How The World Works. When Comey, Clapper and Brennan began their dirty tricks campaign, they could not foresee that it would be so mindlessly overdone as to make itself obvious to all but the most dedicated anti-freedom progressives.

Lesson unlearned, they then over-cooked the books during the Biden "election" fraud; the degree of deception alone made it stick out.

Note: Do not expect our lib-ral friends to be fazed by facts. Mention that the vote tally for Biden was simply not possible, and you will witness that vapid grin and hear: "I know! Isn't that wonderful?"

FOR THE POPE'S STAND ON LATE/PARTIAL-BIRTH INFANTICIDE, see: "climate change".

ORIGINS OF KERRY-IRAN DEAL

Please don't hurt me. Take my milk money/sneakers/girlfriend/pallets of cash.

POOTEE BIG MISTAKEE

Spike & Spunk stopped by the table to ~~see if I would cave~~ wait for me to cave. I was down to the broccoli, <u>and they ate it</u>.

Who knew? Anyway, try convincing the Company that "it was the cats". (Cats, you see, don't step outside to "check the gate".) ps: Don't nobody got laid that night.

CYCLES

Q: How is it that on the same day you can fear everything and fear nothing?

A: Amazing grace: the presence (or absence) of it.

Hot Tip: Doing the right thing always makes you fearless.*
Now, do the math

*OK, "fearless" is not quite accurate. Try: aware of danger, but pissed-off enough to get as crazy as necessary. Do-dah.

I LIKE MY HOODIE. I JUST CRANK UP THE A/C. -Libral TV Commentator

They check your car's carbon footprint, but keep their rental apartment 80° in winter and 70° in summer. (Look for logic elsewhere.) They let their half-dozen rugrats (deposited by a half-dozen absentee baby daddy) play video games clad in shorts/T-shirts/no fucking sox in winter 'counta they get "energy assistance", doncha know. Every autumn the (name withheld) power company sends a flyer astin' me to donate to this madness along with my monthly bill payment. To get my attention, they showed an impeccable Mom (no tattoos, no piercings, no ciggie-butt dangling from collagen lips) reading to (Swear to God) her attentive son (so far, so schmaltz) who is clad in, you guessed it, a T-shirt. One letter like the one you are reading later, the flyer featured a bundled-up, babushka'd, 99 year-old holocaust survivor huddling in her hovel in Siberia. See? Duke Energy reads their mail. (Oops.)

GILLIBRAND (WHERE'S KIRSTEN?) GLOSSARY: **Yuppie Broad**

So, hugs tree, supports sanctuary shit on sidewalks/snuggies in streams?

So, praises PETA, wants border open to devils who fight dogs and roosters?

So, wants all animal shelters "no kill"; abortion after viable baby can cry?

THE TOP BRASS SUCKS, BUT RANK-AND-FILE FBI AGENTS ARE SWELL

Bullshit. These are not the G-Men of yore. They are politically-correct affirmative-action projects who swat-teamed an old man (Roger Stone) at 05:00 for a white collar crime. I watched them in action as they took out a hospital for cooking its books. As they captured the felonious filing cabinets, FBI agents strutted around in black caps with "FBI" in too-large letters and black T-shirts bearing "FBI" in way too-large letters. Most had strings hanging from their shirt sleeves...Oh, wait. That was their arms. These posers never, ever got to school with their milk money; they now revel in their new-found pocket change. Do they suck up to the Establishment? Bro. They <u>are</u> the Establishment.

"ALL THINGS ARE READY IF OUR MINDS BE SO."
-<u>Henry V</u> by Guillermo Shakespeare

When my lovely latina provided me with an approximation of her address, I was reminded of why larger, better-armed Spanish ships never, ever prevailed over smaller English vessels. The latin mind is imprecise.

(Plus, they are never, ever ready.)

THOUGHT PO-LICE

A charity asked for a donation, starting, "Your support matters". I turned them in to BLM.

JUST SAY, "NO THANK YOU"

Cashier: Would you like to round up your purchase to support crippled children (breast cancer research, animal shelters, whatever)?

Yuppie: So, not today?

Translation: "I authorized up to 99¢ last time." (She didn't.)

(pick one) "I will authorize up to 99¢ next time." (She won't.)

OUR KIDS, OUR SAY

Outsiders crashing your school board meetings? Reguire local ID. Dumbass.

Note: The same bespectacled undoable shows up in Seattle, Portland and Peoria. Pray she never breeds. **Editrix**: Oh, I think she's safe.

FREEDOM OF NO CHOICE

Q: What should we do if the Democrat senate candidates win in Georgia?

A: Impeach them the same day.

Q: What should we do if the Republican senate candidates win in Georgia?

A: Impeach them the same day.

Q: Weren't Perdue and Loeffler cleared by their Senate colleagues?

Oh, right. And Ted Bundy was cleared by the Manson family.

Q: Has there ever been a sleazier Senator?

A: A: Chances are 99 out of 100.

PREACHER'S PRIORITIES

The padre prattled that we should keep our decorations up for the entire Christmas season, which runs 'till the Epiphany, a week or so into January. Tell me, priest, how many babies will be late-term/partial-birth aborted during that time?

WHY NOT GET ONE LESS TATTOO/PIERCING AND HAVE FLUFFY FIXED?

"Way-ell, Moma Kay-et done did it agin!" Her conscience is clear: she brings them to the shelter. Any being that can pretend that partial-birth abortion is not murder can make believe that she is not really telling the overwhelmed county shelter, "Here. Kill these kittens for me. Agin.", just as her kin have no qualms about setting a box o' kitties in an empty lot. After all, they left an old blanket and a day's worth of table scraps. "Thee Babble say-es God gave man dominion..."

"NO MORE 'AMERICA FIRST'! YAY!"

It took your mainstream "news" media two days to realize that this is not what most Americans want to hear. I guess Wolf, Jake and Dana/Andrea will fall back to, "Yay! No more V.A. reform, favorable trade deals, energy independence, or pardoning blacks who were over-sentenced by Obiden policies."

R U THAT STUPID?

"Thomas Lewis fought for civil rights before I was born. Vote for me. I'm John Ossoff."

PONCE' DE LEON, MOVE OVER

My vet has discovered the Fountain of Youth, and she doesn't even live in Florida. This is beginning to annoy me.

YUPPIES WERE TAUGHT "NEW MATH" and "APPROX-IMATE SPELLING". Thank a teechr.

Purina Pro Plan Veterinary Supplements Hydra Care Feline Hydration Supplement requires "2 oz/5 lbs of body weight daily". It comes, of course, in 3 oz. pouches.

Dose quickly became a non-issue when my diabetic/arthritic/geriatric Brat ~~declined~~ refused it, so I tried it on the others. Ethne growled. Grant wet himself. Spudly tried to bite me. Max calmly (too calmly, I thought) brought out a box of .22 shorts.

A taste test told the tale. I flush nicer things down my toilet.

LIB-RAL LEXICON

You may say, "Come celebrate our abortions with us" (You think I am making this up, don't you?) at the Million Mengele Moms March.*

You may not say, "American exceptionalism", an obvious racist dogwhistle, according to our progressive thought police.

*300,000 pro-infanticide hoydens equals "A Million Moms".

300,000 pro-life people equals "over 1,000 protesters",

Yes, CNN, 300,000 is "over 1,000", so your reporting is statistically accurate but very, very fake.

pms: Short of crapping on po-lice cars, the Million Murderous Moms & Man-Buns left behind as much filth as any Earth Day celebration/shitfest.

SO, MORE YUPPIESPEAK?

So, their 47-year fraud hasn't even been installed yet, and the left is already Finding Ways to spend Other People's Money (yours) to emasculate middle-eastern men? So, women's rights without borders? So, bored with the man-buns they created here, they feel a need to fuck up another society somewhere else? So, hear me roar?

Q: So, why do you think they're finished here?

A: So, we work two jobs while our man-bun (or "wife") sits our spawn?

Q: So, do you miss the nuclear family?

A: So, no? So, one job pays for daycare? So, the other job covers essentials (tattoos, piercings, ciggies, beer, mani-pedis, extensions)?

Q: So, how do you buy food?

A: So, we don't, silly? So, the dumbass taxpayers provide groceries and (get this) "energy assistance"? So, we keep our thermostat pegged up in winter (kids play Dungeons & Dragons barefoot) and cranked down in summer?

Q: So, that's Where Do The Children Play (Cat Stevens)? So, I guess I shouldn't ask what they learn at school?

A: So, the gov-mint has that all figured out? So, something called "core-something"? So, I am sooo over this, totally? So, my group chat at Starbucks...

HEY, AT LEAST GRAHAM

Didn't vote for millions of your money to end paternalism in Pakistan... Oops!

LINSEY'S LEGACY

Mommy! Mommy! What does the ~~dishwasher~~ $enator do?

Smiles with Trump: asks U.S. for money.

Alone with Pelosi: asks her what to do.

Q: What has been Trump's biggest impediment?

A: The (whore) House and the (sleazy) Senate.

Q: How sleazy can a $enate candidate be?

A: Lookit the race in Georgia.

Q: Republican or Democrat?

A: Yes.

Q: What are the chances that your $enator is sleazy?

A: 99 out of 100.

Q: Mommyl Mommy! What does "tits on a bull" mean?

A: Now child, that would be the House and the $enate. Oh, and the Supreme Court.

Q: How useless were the swamp $enators to the first populist President since TR?

A: Haven't you been paying attention? Tits on a bull. see: NeverTrumpers

Q: What will we be when China takes U.S. over?

A: Better off.

OVARIES

The lids for her egg-size/shape tupperware have all been lost, so today's I Am Strong woman has Found Yet Another Way to avoid the drudgery of p-p-peeling an egg. This time it is a giant plastic egg that incubates its charges in the microwave. Yay! No more pesky building a fire...excuse me, turning a knob on the stove to b-b-boil some water. No siree, B-B-Roberta. Five easy payments. Hear Me Roar.

pms: Support your egg fetish. Source www.ovarian sis.com to explore an online tutorial.

Coming soon from Toyota: The 2021 Priaprius. warranted to gestate your ova for you in 9 months/9,000 miles. Man-bun not included. See your organic midwife/mechanic for details. Butterflies & unicorns. Coalition. Birkenstock. Earth.

LIKE SELLING CORNWATER WITH CLYDESDALES

Polyseamseal has the best caulking and the worst salespersons. The inverse is true of Dap products & people. Dap is as ubiquitous as it is awful; Polyseamseal is, alas, unobtainium.

BRAVE NEW WORLD ORDER GLOBAL GREEN COVID DEAL GODSEND FOR THE LEFT COALITION

Capitalism centers half the wealth among the very rich. Let's replace it with Obidenism, which places all the wealth among the very rich. Relax: everyone else gets put on the gov-mint dole. What's that? You still have some self-respect and want to work for a living? Pshaw! The dignity of honest labor? Tee, hee. Now be good boys & girls, go back inside, and put on your masks.

Q: IF COVID DIDN'T exist, would China have invented it?

A: They did. see: mail-in ballot fraud resulting in Obiden. Dumbass.

OVAR E-Z (REPRISE). HOW DO YOU LIKE YOUR EGGS?

Peeling an egg confuses her. Do not give her a rifle. Or, of course, bleach.

Q: When will egg cookers shaped like giant ovaries be marketed to men?

A: When men start hanging blindingly shiny objects on their rearview mirrors*, covering one eye with their hair, and wearing shirts that button in the back.

*Aw, to be blinded, you'd have to, like, look at it.

DADS ARE OPTIONAL. ASK ANY PROGRESSIVE.

I wondered why I wasn't more frightened when I slapped a pistol out of the punk's hand. Then I remembered how I felt the day I broke Father's lifetime fishing rod while playing with it. After that, all fear became relative.

ps: Sis said, "Quick, go hide". Mother came out, saw the look on my face, told me to stay put, and went back inside to give Dad a heads-up. I heard her say something that sounded like, "You probably shouldn't kill him". Too soon, up steps His Hugeness. He examines the rod and says, "Look right here, Son; it was damaged already". Next day, he bought a new pole and took me fishing. Advantage: nuclear family.

Attention anti-family BLM Marxist "Hands up, don't shoot" liars*, anti-family LGBT-QRS (WTF?) thugs, and anti-family radical feminists: Go fuck yourselves.

*Surprise! The left seized on a shooting to mobilize spoiled brat/useful idiots as rioters, then blamed Trump for "divisiveness". Hot Tip: Taking out Michael Brown was way past justified; it was a community service.

DOCTORAL SYN-THESIS

Q: Did Jill really give a high school dropout 50 bucks and say, "Write me something about something; just make it eat paper"?

A: No, silly; it just reads that way.

Q: When does a Doctor of Education become a Medical Doctor?

A: When she goes on The View.*

Q: Is anybody in Family Biden not a fraud?

A: Not so you'd notice.

*Don't nobody there know the dif'rence, nohow. see: very new money

CNN/DNC

Q: Doesn't Biden's refusal to take questions annoy journalists?

A: These aren't journalists; they are operatives.

Q: Wouldn't this furtiveness cause them to question their...cause?

A: Dontcarehatetrump.

MOTTO

State Department: Piss on my neck? Thanks for the rain. Take some U.S. money.

Obama Presidency: As above, with an apology.

Biden Presidency: I will not declare until all my votes are counted.

Democratic Party: Vote early, vote late, vote often.

3 KIDS IN PRIVATE SCHOOL, 2 IN PUBLIC
Guess how they vote?
ps: The private schoolers can tell you <u>why</u>.

SO, UNITED STATES ARMY

OF WAIFS SECTION?

(SO, IN YUPPIESPEAK?)

No soldier wants to wake up and see a pair of size 5 boots under the next bunk.

"I didn't join the Army (A-r-m-y, dumbass) to fight. I joined the Army (A-r-m-y, dumbass) to get a degree so I could teach kindergarten." -the "waif" that Delta Force risked life & limb to rescue during Desert Storm. *

So, it's hard to care about a nation of obedients who speak in questions?

So, when China finds out what Obiden has given them, they will give it back?

So, the Army (A-r-m-y, dumbass) will fight them off with 90 lb. soldierettes?

So, (approved pronouns), if you are not feeling icky, bloated, or horrid, please person your weapons? So, there is a solution? So, a battalion of bull dykes? So, we'll give them bad haircuts, tell them they're fat, and put them in SUVs? So, them Chinamen will run away?

*So, the NYT called the little tyke a "waif" and immediately regretted it when Christiane Amanpour jumped on them with both hairy legs?

SO, IS IT EVEN WORTH SAVING?

Throughout history, nations have given up their freedom for safety.

Today, half your Country gave it up for politically-correct pronouns.

IN CASE OF NORMAL

Att TV commercial companies: Why not craft an ad designed for deplorables? How 'bout a not same-sex, not bi-racial, not trans-gender couple wherein the person who identifies with the male gender is allowed to drive the car. You just might could get some irredeemables to source your product, and not just for theysells; shucks, they might would gift it to they yuppie naybors. Y'all.

THE SCOPE OF IT

If forward-thinking evolution occurs, the inverse must also be true. This explains our flat faces. Throughout the eons, no dog, deer, opossum, gnu, wallaby, whatever ever did the same stupid shit, over and over, then slapped itself on the forehead and said, "Zxcvbnm lkjhgfdsai", which is caveman for, "What was I thinking!" This, and only this, explains why, over and over, human beings vote-in a Party that has promised to enslave them. "But...but...they'll keep our free shit a-comin'...Aw (Whap!), what was I thinking!"

FUCKED UP

Trump was criminalized for using indelicate language. The House leader who said, "We'll have to pass this Bill (ACA) to see what's in it" is still in office. Not to harp, but this does not sound like a people worth saving.

MORE FUCKED UP

No matter how many countries Socialism has sucked the soul out of, the left wants to try it again, over and over. This <u>defines</u> insanity.

INAUGURATION

To deny Trump the slight of sending his VP, CNN fake-reported, "Pence said he'd go".

MIND ROT

Flippin' through channels has its dangers. Passing by MTV or VH-1, one is accosted by fat, ugly men dressed as caricatures of fat, ugly women. Trying to unsee that shit, you'll come across a Teen Moron Mom asking her toddler for permission to dip fries in her milk, too ("Is it good? Can I try it?") and the bitch <u>is already breeding.</u> This is scary shit. Meanwhile, I'm being told which pronouns to use. A society worth saving? You decide. I'm over it.

MTV responds: "Dude. Send kids what message? Anyway, Bro, black lives matter."

TAKE THE TV. THEY HAVE INSURANCE.

Insurance works by spreading the risk among those who buy it. When BLM/ANTIFA rioted in liberal-run cities, your homeowners and/or business insurance was bound to go up 50-100 bucks. Because lib-ral mayors and governors allowed the "mostly peaceful protests" of the Summer of Love to go on for months, your bill went up $468 or more. The only justice in this is that lib-rals pay more, too.

IMPOTENCE

The Big Tech companies who control the dissemination of information were starting to censor conservative thought, so they were requested (but not required) to appear before the $enate. Surprisingly, they showed up, and were asked a series of stern questions by several $enators, many of whom shook their $enatorial $ubsidy fingers at them. The result: Big Tech now censors all conservative thought. Christ, Cruz musta scared the crap outta them.

Why, next thing you know, they'll be censoring the President of the United States... Oops!

Note: 100 years ago, the U.S.S.R began by controlling all information.

Ask your tenured hoax to look it up for you. Dumbass.

GROTESQUE GOVERNMENTS GET GOD WROTH: BYE-BYE COUNTRY

Ancient Rome	Modern America
blood sports: wild animal fighting	blood sports: dog & cock fighting*
killing of innocents: Christians	killing of innocents: late abortions
lead water pipes	aluminum beverage cans
unbeatable army unfunded when society crumbled	unbeatable Army ruined by politics as society crumbled
suffered $enator $ubsidies	suffered $enator $ubsidies

*The left imports indigents who are certain to vote Democrat. The Archbishops harbor fugitives who are certain to be Catholic. Being brown blind (and NFL fans), Peta and Greenpeace are silent on American blood sports, which are now practiced by whites & blacks. Thanks, Archbishopric.

**P.C. turned a fighting machine into a social experiment. Thanks, Hillary.

Preachers prattled, parishioners preened. Nobody stopped late-term/partial-birth infanticide. The blood, sweat and tears of all our patriots could not atone for this ultimate evil. Against all logic, America's reckoning is here.

ASK ANY HIGH SCHOOL ~~STU~~ ATTENDEE WHICH CAME FIRST:

Charlemagne or Coca Cola. Then ask its NEA teacher. Do-dah.

CHOCOLATE CHASTITY BELT

The TV ad showed her eyes rolling back in her head, so I got The Girl a buncha "Sweet Desire Dark" and "Deep wishes with Nuts" before I went out of town for a week. The neighbors said she never left the house.

COVID COMPLIANT

I fashioned a facemask the first time Fauci flip-flopped on its efficacy, and I've been wearing it ever since.

efficacy: Don't nobody know what it means, but it sounds important. Kinda like saying "dentifrice" when you mean "tooth-paste". see: a charlatan's go-to word. from: Fauci's First Faux Fact-book (www.weasel.com)

CATECHISM

Catholic Church: universal belief. Islam wanted to become universal, too.

- They didn't use similar methods. Oops!

- Holy Mother Church finally quit this shit, so the Protes-tants took over. Look it up.

Papa Francisco: universal dislike.

NOT UNDECIDED VOTER
Conservative: Do you want the American people or China to decide this election?

Liberal: I want this election decided against Trump.

MORE MIND ROT
Forgetting that the new kid was a product of Liberalism 101: Basic Brainwashing, I remarked that (most) women don't read road signs while (most) men do. He was shocked that I saw a d-d-difference 'tween women & men. When I offered proof via the fact that chicks are the ones you see pulled right up to the barrier begging to be let in, having ignored two fucking miles of "lane closed" signs, he fell back on his training per Liberalism 201: Never, Ever Let Facts Stop You From Toeing The Politically-Correct Lib-ral Line.

Editrix: So that's why I say, "Get off at the Saks exit" and my sweet-but-studly author will tell you to "take exit 467". Who knew? ps: My main man is somewhat of a wizard. Not only can he say that exit 467 is 9 miles from exit 476 (How does he do that?), he can (get this) he can face north and tell you that east is to his right and west is on his left. SEXISM ALERT: No fair introducing "left" and "right".

Note: The most illiterate 14 year-old blue water jack tar on any ocean-going sailing vessel could box the compass while skylarking in the rigging. Arithmetic held no terrors for him. He commanded a basic knowledge of world, yes, world* geography and, since this was B.C. (Before Computers), he had the ability to think. Compare this to today's NEA-indoctrinated dolts who ask their momma for new Nikes at age 20. Again, not to harp, but is it worth saving?

*Yep. B.F.G. (Before Fucking Google), he knew that South America was not "like, Alabama and stuff". Dumbass.

PER CNN

Private Big Tech can cancel free speech. Cool. Bakers can now cancel same-sex wedding cakes.

GALA
TYPO SECTION
#######

W HY BAXTER HANGED HIMSELF...OOPS!

Dexter	**Baxter**
History D-	History A
Geography F	Geography A+
Math F	Math A
Science F	Science B+
Deportment F	Deportment A

"The School Board accepts responsibility for the typo but not the hanging."

ps: Did momma sue? You bet. Since she had already taken a million bucks in

dissembled disability, energy assistance and, of course, free phones for

her offspring 'time they was 6 (they be 12 o' them), it was a wash.

Note: At the Foodway, I saw an EBT cardholder shoulder a sack of rice...<u>kidding.</u>

YOUR REPRESENTATIVES AT WORK
Covid relief bill: 6 months
Trump impeachment: 6 hours

THERE GO THE WOMEN'S VOTE
Dems'll pay a price for impeachment II; they...they pre-empted Judge Judy.

SPARKLES/SUCKS
Walmart's has great prices and in-store service. Their phone customer service sucks. The Pakistani who says her name is "Heather" (Gee, d'ya think they offshore some jobs?) cannot understand you, nor you her, so she puts on a Phil Collins/Sheryl Crowe song so you'll hang up. Not wanting that shit in your head all day, you do.

ANIMAL CONTROL
Ya can't shoot the cat for using the water dish as a foot bath, but don't tell him that. ps: If he doesn't know what a .22 is, show him the vacuum.

PELOSI PERFIDY
Antifa: "People do what they do."
Capitol: "Impeach Trump!"

LIB-RAL LOGIC

Racist: whites are smarter because they have less melanin.

Not racist: Biacks are smarter because they have more melanin.

p(m)s: Guess who Obiden hired to oversee race relations.

DEMOCRAT: LIBERAL PARTY OF TOLERANCE AND DIVERSITY.

Watch me tear up the elected opposition's speech.

FAT CAT DOESN'T EAT HIS FOOD: HE ADDRESSES IT

Steps up to his bowl, he does, and sets-up with a little wiggle like a golfer fixin' to putt. Did I mention he is fat?

Editrix: "FAT". We just got tooken down from Big Tech media. Dumbass.

BACHELOR TIP 27

Told The Girl I'd pay for her haircut. Dumbass. Seems as since she was Right There, she got it colored as well. While they tinted her tresses, a mani-pedi seemed to be in order and, when they were not quite finished, she hauled off and got a dermal abrasion. (Who wouldn't?) Ever-efficient with her time, she had the mobile car care criminal detail everything on her ride save the bottom of the tires. Here come The Tip: when presented The Bill for all this madness, resist the urge to blurt, "Christ, I coulda called in two 18 year-olds".

Trust me on this one. Dumbass.

DO-OVER

Blueheads can't wait to see their grandkids. The children <u>they</u> raised: notsomuch.

NO FAIRNESS NEEDED

Tainted victory? Pshaw! No one could ever accuse CNN of not gloating.

DA BA DA BA DA BA DA BA...SOLD!

Selling the Pelosis a car must be fun.

Q: Is it a 6 or an 8?

A: You have to buy it to see what it has.

Q: Are the seats cloth or leather?

A: Pay attention: You have to buy it to see Whiskey Tango Foxtrot's innit.

ps: Nancy hada accept the deal, since she expected U.S. to.

DOUBLE NO-STANDARD

If the lib-ral establishment likes you, your feral fretting first lady will be All Over the fashion magazines. If the lib-ral establishment hates your guts, your elegant, sharp-dressed, Eurasian-eyed/foreign-born (Diversity?) beauty will be shunned by all. <u>Obedience</u>!

Note: I said, "feral", you thought, "Michelle". Anybody would. It's the eyes.

GILLIBRAND (WHO?) GLOSSARY: "SMARMY"- YOU WIPED WHEN YOU SHOULD HAVE WASHED

Q: When lib-rals so viciously turn on their own, as when Bill Smarmy Mahr stated the obvious ("Islam sucks"), why don't their own leave the fold?

A: Sheeple.

<u>ARTHUR</u> miscast Minelli as a shoplifting trollop when Streisand was Right There.

DACHSHUNDS ARE ABLE, TOO; AND <u>TOUGH</u>: 'Nother Clinton crony got his head ate off... by his wiener dog. <u>Able</u>.

KIDZ

My Daughter has deemed her Dad a dolt in matters hi-tech, but the joke's on her. Father knows wut up. The youngster goes to a photo shop (You have heard of these, no?) and finds a foto of an athletic* chick looks like her. (The resemblance is eerie.) Then she selects snowy scenes shot in Big Sky country, pastes the lot onna blank postcard, types a message on the back (Who knew she had a typewriter?), laminates it somehow, and sends it to give the impression that she is snowboarding in Montana. <u>Very</u> trick.

*The "athletic" gave it away; the tyke <u>bounces</u> when she runs and throws like a girl.

Att Olympic Committee: Testing/schmesting; <u>watch it run</u>. If it bounces, cries when it falls or shot-puts a ball, its a chick.

BLM/ANTIFA, EAT YOUR HEART OUT

White privelege is real. All summer of love long, BLM/ANTIFA tried to get the National Guard called on theysells; all summer of love long, they rioted, looted, arsoned and assaulted in vain. 'Long comes the first Trump demo to get out of hand (Aw, did Wolf/Jake/Andrea-Dana forget to mention two busloads of ANTIFA that infiltrated the crowd?) and here come the Guardsmen. Don't tell me there ain't no white privelege. ps: Uh, ignore all those black Trumpsters. Wolf/Jake/Andrea-Dana do.

Note: Cities on fire, Mom & Pop businesses smashed, infrastructure ruined, and the best BLM/ANTIFA can do is get called "mostly peaceful protesters". <u>It is not their fault</u>. These pussies lacked the Trumpsters secret weapon: the Red Hat. Why, everybody knows that "Make America Great Again" is secret Skinhead/Dogwhistle/Code for "Kill Black People". Shit. They might as well shout "All Lives Matter" at a BLM/ANTIFA rally.

Gillibrand (Remember her? Neither do I.) Glossary

riot: Lost to language during the summer of love. Re-invented on 1/6/21 and used twice a minute ever since on CNN/DNC.

WHAT SORT OF MAN ~~READS PLAYBOY~~ VOTES BIDEN?

An able man. Able to forget that Trump was still talking when his speech "incited" an ANTIFA-instigated riot that was planned by John Sullivan (ask his brother; CNN won't) weeks earlier. Also able to say, "Trump's wall fell down" when two (2) old-style panels (Trump updated/upgraded these) were prematurely placed on uncured concrete footings. Also able to pretend that the wall did not cut illegal invasion by 80%. I mean, this guy is <u>able</u>.

Note: Trump's new-style wall panels solved the drainage problems created by the boneheaded solid ones and allow our Border Patrol agents to see what in the Good Christ (excuse me, Angie) is going on t'other side.

ABLE ADDENDA: ABLE to believe that Vince Foster shot himself with the wrong hand and rolled himself in a rug, that the Park Police were the best Hillary choice to investigate this, that polaroid (no film) photos were lost, that Ruby Ridge/Waco folks posed a threat to national security, that the best way to save the kids from "abuse" was to kill them, that 6' Jeff Epstein hanged himself from a 5' bunk while both guards were on break at the same time. <u>Able</u>.

TRUE BUT FAKE: If 300,000 Right to Lifers is "over a thousand", two (2) panels means "Trump's wall fell down".

GALA
HARRIET HOUSEWIFE
SUZY HOMEMAKER
JUNE CLEAVER
SECTION

NON-COMPARISON SHOPPING
Since fool-resistant ("low splash") and scented bleaches are not used for emergency water purification, Clorox is not required to tell you the percentage of sodium hypochlorite, so they don't.

KVETCHING OVER SPILLED MILK
Save rinsing a rag. Use a motorized contraption (But... But it's cordless!). Now you have two things to clean. Dumbass.

R-R-RINSE A R-R-RAG? PART II

Yuppie broads wonder what died two days after Bisseling up a milk spill. Dumbass.

THEM DEMS

November Nancy

Got plenty votes in NY. Let's send some to PA where it's close. Sure, China who will own U.S., but we have to change this racist Country we all hate.

January Jerrold

BLM/ANTIFA rioted all summer of love, but one opposition rally turned violent (by BLM/ANTIFA agitators) means we must impeach Trump to save this wonderful Country we all love.

Vatican Vibes

It Takes A Pope To Run A Village -Pro-Abortion Catholic President

I USED T0 BE A REPUBLICAN AND OTHER DEFLECTIONS

Impeachment II Day. Hadn't seen her in years. She led off with, "Trump pinched women on the ass, parodied a paralytic and...and his wall fell down"*. Wow! The gal is a genius. Finally, someone has explained why we gave up our freedom of speech and helped China run our industry into the ground. (Note to self: crip derides you and your family, do not mock back.) She threw in the standard, "I used to be a Republican". Makes sense. Once you hook up with a disability scam/welfare weasel, remaining Republican is "like buying drugs from a priest: it just doesn't feel right"**. Note: A racer once gave this corner worker an action photo signed, "To K: I'd know you in a flash", a reference to her fetish for flashing her tits*** as the guys sped by Turn 2. Now she feigns outrage 'cause private citizen Trump pinched a butt. Q: Is this irony or hypocrisy? A: Yes.

*When two (2) stupid solid panels tipped, Trump had the thing re-designed to allow drainage and visibility. Google, of course, says, "Trump's wall fell down" and, CNN-style, omitted that it continues to reduce invasion by 80%.

**Tommy Tiernan ***I paid for one of those.

ps: I used to be a Republican, too. Now I'm a RIRO (Republican In Registration Only) so I can help primary <u>every</u> incumbent out, <u>any</u> newcomer in. They could hardly do worse.

NOVEMBER 4, 2020: The Trump flag stayed up. The In God We Trust sign came down.

PURGING TRUMP: WHO is more afraid of a popular president; establishment Democrats or entrenched Republicans? Yes.

FOOD COURT (YOU BE THE JUDGE)
Wouldn't the Mall be better served by a Traffic Court?
Q: Why are apple turnovers sprinkled with sugar and aquarium gravel?
A: And cherry turnovers.
Q: Why does bee pollen taste like dirt?
A: Because it is.

Q: What exactly is tofu?

A: Tojam.

TEAM BIDEN BABIES SOLDIERS

Joe hunkers them by their Hum-Vees; Jill carts them cookies. Sheesh. Republican swamp creatures at least bring pizza.

Q: Why are the Guardsmen there?

A: So they can't respond to BLM/ANTIFA.

Hearing that they were quartered on concrete, the red states brought them home.

Q: Why not the blue states?

A: So they would be fed with O.P.M., silly. (Other People's Money)

PLUG THE PIPE, PAVE THE PLANET

Progressives hate pipes, but why? Pipes rarely run themselves aground on rocky shores and almost never collide with ships (or other pipes) or catch fire and/or explode. Pesky fact: caribou fawns frolic under the Alaska pipe; surely Bambi will return to the Trudeau tube. Do You want To Know A Secret? (Do-Da-Do) You may say I'm a dreamer, but Imagine how much fossil fuel a tanker burns in coupla weeks to deliver as much oil as a pipe does in a day.

Q: Would you want Uber to arrive in a double bus?

A: Dontcarehatetrump.

Q: Want your grubhub organic tofu/sesame pizza delivered by tractor-trailer?

A: Dontcarehatetrump.

Q: Wanna sacrifice your future/nation/planet for a…(sorry)…a pipe dream?

A: Dontcarehatetrump.

Q: How 'bout we paint the pipe green?

A: Why didn't you say so? Fucking kumbaya, Dude!

Editrix: Purging The Pipe is the fastest way for Obiden to apologize for U.S. and our energy independence <u>and</u> surrender a strategic resource to our good friends in Saudi Arabia, Iran, Russia and China. Just ask Jen.

ps: Wanna keep the pipe? Piece of yuppiecake. Simply donate every billionth barrel to the Birkenstock Organic Moonbeam Natural Coalation Earth Gluten-free Macrame Sea Salt Solar Shelter For Saving Green Hispanic Lesbian Whales.

GILLIBRAND (WHO?) GLOSSARY

"Oriental" means you are from the Orient and is somehow racist.

"Asian" means you are from Asia (the Orient) and is somehow not racist.

"Tillerman", "foretopman", "Englishman/Frenchman" are OK; "Chinaman" is definitely not OK. If this makes sense to you, please vote Democrat.

THE MADE IN CHINA TOOTHBRUSH SUCKED,
so I hauled off and bought a Colgate. It was made in China.

######
MISOGEN...
MYSOG...
SEXISM MADE EASY
SECTION

ENVIRONMENTALIST KORNER -CNN/DNC
Objecting to job exportation is sooo racist. Everybody knows that third world hellholes are just as concerned as we are about thoughtful logging/forest replenishment, careful mining and drilling, treating tannery and paper mill effluent, etc. Butterflies & rainbows. Kumbaya.

Editrix: Bounty and Yoplait Yogurt animal traps should be Hecho en Honduras so chicks...I mean, strong women everywhere won't have to r-r-rinse a rag, and will be able to say, "Awww" each and every time they see baby mammals slowly strangling/suffocating to death in cutesy backwards containers that were designed just for them. Hear me roar.

PENIS ENVY REPLACED BY OVARIAN OBSESSION -CNN/D&C

In that seat of knowledge, learning and invention known as West (and East and Central) Africa, mighty women have Found A Way to avoid p-p-peeling an egg by using a giant microwaveable ovum, if only they could find a place to p-p-plug it. pms: The little plastic ova were discharged within five (5) days of discovering that their use required Miss Thing to b-b-boil water.

APOLOGY ACCEPTED

Q: When was the Amazon Desert called the Amazon Rainforest?

A: Before Obiden apologized for American jobs and sent them overseas.

FOILED AGAIN

She puts the pretty side out and blinks at you when told that the unfinished aspect now faces the food. Thus clad, the potato resists an hour of baking (reflection, doncha know), so do not expect her to boil the oldest eggs for easy p-p-peeling. I can't wait to hand her a loaded rifle...<u>kidding</u>.

REPEATING HISTORY

Next time you see our pussified police putting out flag fires instead of arresting the louts who lit them, consider this:

As their country crumbled, ancient Romans viewed mind-rotting spectacles.

Today's Americans watch Teen Moron Mom and The View.

Ancient Romans imported blood sports including cock and dog fighting.

Lib-ral Americans import people who engage in cock and dog fighting.

Vandals and Goths pulled down Roman statues, destroyed buildings and stole stuff.

We permit BLM/ANTIFA to do likewise because we tremble at being called "racist".

A has-been nation of pussies? You decide.

LIB-RAL: HAVING REPEATED the last string of "news" stories that were proven to be false, he/she/undecided will parrot the next flush of "news" stories that will be proven to be false with arrogance and condescension, absent explanation or embarrassment. Pointing this out will garner a, "Not necessarily" or, "I thought you were smarter than that" or some equally compelling argument.

IMPRACTICAL JOEKSTER

Sal, Murr, Joe and Q need to tell each other to "Salute the Marines".

BALLROOM

Stretched-out briefs not providing support? Double 'em up.

Q: Doesn't your crotch get hot?

A: Depends on what I'm thinking.

DIVIDIN' BIDEN

In the interest of "equity", let U.S. fire every black mayor of every city that is less than 51% black. Reparations to the whites who were forced to live under this systemic racism are in order. Executive order.

ADVENTURES IN MOVING

All you oil drillers can get new jobs capping wells. -President Biden

You can make solar panels; you might have to move. -Please Don't Hurt Me Kerry

Q: Won't China make the panels?

A: Bro. The man said you might have to move.

BLATANT

CNN gave Trump a Covid Counter Corner of the TV screen. I guess they don't like Biden as much. Note: No lib-ral has asked for it back. How odd.

Q: Do they suddenly not want to know?

A: Know what?

THE PEOPLE'S BUSINESS

Sure, we'll get you a stimulus check, after we impeach outgoing Trump.

IT WAS THE FINEST YOUTH GROUP ON THE PLANET, SO <u>IT HAD TO GO</u>.

Held in abject fear of political correctness, you and your countrymen let LGBT-WTF thugs infiltrate the BSA, which then had to be shut down due to (Surprise!) pedophilia. As always, suppression of a people starts with cowing them, and U.S. did. We deserve Family Biden and fucking Jen Psaki. Dumbass.

ps: A Scout is Trustworthy, Loyal, Helpful, Friendly, Courteous, Kind, Obedient, Cheerful, Thrifty, Brave, Clean and Reverent. Of course they had to be destroyed. Note: Knowing they are next, the Girl Scouts have been damn silent. !No te preoccupes! The young ladies can go to Teen Moron Moms for guidance.

ON THE PLUS SIDE...

"The Americans did it!" -CCP. Even though they helped engineer the takeover of the USA, The People's Redundant Republic of Communist Fucking China didn't think US were quite that dumb*. Seeing how easy it was, they may not want US.

*Obviously, they never met an NEA (union, no competency testing) teacher.

*THIRD WORLD FOOD ANIMAL

Anything that crawls. The lucky ones are killed; many are cooked alive. Kumbaya.

SLOW LEARNERS

Maine potato ~~farmers~~ agribusinessmen Pshaw!-d the millenia-old practices of crop rotation/field resting, which is why Maine potatoes now taste like the worn-out dirt they are grown in. Much of the potato industry shifted to the excellent soil of Idaho, where ~~farmers~~ agribusinessmen Pshaw!-d the millenia-old practices of crop rotation/field resting, which is why Idaho potatoes now taste like the worn-out dirt they are grown in.

Q: Don't they add chemicals to the worn-out soil to make stuff grow?

A: OK, your potato glows in the dark; it still tastes like dirt.

Note: As elsewhere, hedgerows were removed to facilitate planting/harvesting with colossal combines. With nothing to stop wind & water soil erosion, a new dustbowl era awaits the next drought. This, of course, will be blamed on Trump, who doubtless caused the one in 1929. Do-dah.

ps: Florida's excellent soil ain't worn out yet, but they workin' onnit.

Editrix: Medieval ~~agribesinessmen~~ farmers augmented crop alternation with the three field system, which left one field fallow in yearly rotation. More food was raised on the remaining two fields than would be grown on three fields of worn-out soil, a real consideration when using a single-bottom animal-drawn plow. Biden's war on oil may bring it back.

Q: The war on oil will return U.S. to dark ages farming?

A: Heavens, no. We won't have an animal to pull the plow.

If you doubt this, visit oil-rich Venezuela. Dumbass.

THE SEXES ARE NOT EQUAL (NO SHIT)

No man has ever learned to f-f-fold a fitted sheet. On t'other hand, why would we? It's gonna end up on the bed, so why f-f-fold and store it? Two-three layers of high thread count, what's the difference? Likewise the pillow cases. You have tear-offs on your race helmet faceshield, no? Expect no less from your bed. That way, when you trick the New Girl to enter your abode, you don't even have to think about whether the hair/makeup will match. Simply wait 'till she's in the bathroom*, snatch that shit off, and toss it inna closet- Hot Tip: while you're attit, check for barrettes and bobby pins that were left there, and in the couch, on purpose. Note: This is entry-level stuff. Protect yourself. Find the glass with the lipstick on it that you never saw the old New Girl use, and for heaven's sake, wipe the nail polish scrapings off the inside of the refrigerator handle.

*Hope you checked your medicine cabinet. She will.

ps: If she says she's, "In law enforcement"...

Do Not: Run to flush all the toilets as a joke.

But Do: Resist the urge to say, "So, you tidied-up and fetched the coffee?"

Trust me on this one.

PIPE DREAM

Too late to paint The Pipe green; the know-nothings have already cancelled it. Relax. The third world will handle oil production just as carefully as we did. Why, lookit how nicely they perform their logging, leather tanning, sewage treatment, etc., and how humanely they raise and slaughter their food animals.*

Butterflies & Birkenstocks & Rainbows & Unicorns & Sea Salt & Macramé & Kumbaya.

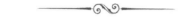

VICARS OF...CHRIST?

The Spanish are deeply religious but strongly anti-clerical. Priest like Father Pflager and Pope Francis remind me why. Note: In Spain, the Holy Inquisition and the Spanish Civil war may have had a tad to do with it.

Your NEA (union, no competency testing) teacher will tell you all about it, or you can ask your Fundamentalisms Of Tax Exemption graduate/pastor.

SMALL BUT SCRAPPY

Wanna learn some unrevised history? Fire your tenured hoax and subscribe to The American Rifleman. Better yet, join the Association that publishes it and get the magazine, insurance, and some political clout for free. Most issues sport at least one article on something historic. The February 2021 edition features a story on World War II (look it up) British Commandos. One photo taken before the Boulogne raid shows that many of these badasses were below average height. Cynics would say they were "overcompensating"; maybe they were bullied as youngsters. Who cares? Look at their calm but determined faces. They didn't go the man-bun route, and nobody's gonna bully them now.

ps: A French resistance fighter I knew was quite small, as were couple guys with numbers tattooed on their wrists. You wouldn't fuck with them, either.

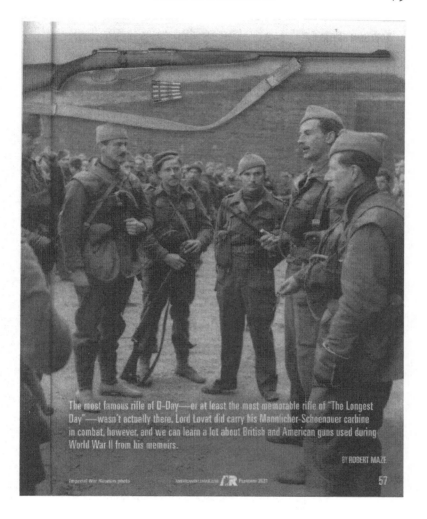

The most famous rifle of D-Day—or at least the most memorable rifle of "The Longest Day"—wasn't actually there. Lord Lovat did carry his Mannlicher-Schoenauer carbine in combat, however, and we can learn a lot about British and American guns used during World War II from his memoirs.

BY ROBERT MAZE

Imperial War Museum photo   57

Also by Phil Berto:
SNIPPETS – COMMENTS FROM THE RED
SNIPPED – AMERICA POST #ME TOO
SNIPS – COMMENTS FROM THE BLACK AND BLUE
SNAPPED – COMMENTS FROM A C-C-CONSERVA-
TIVE
SNAPPER – THE LIBERAL FINGER
UNSNAPPED – OBEDIENT LIB-RAL EDITION
FIVE SLEAZY SLIPPETS AND A MISSIVE OR TWO

PROMOTIONAL (TO OPT out, press Whiskey Tango Foxtrot)

"If I embarrass you, tell your friends." – Belle Barth

If I annoy you, tell your yuppie friends it'll cost 'em $7.77 to find out why. They will, of course, negotiate the price down to 77¢ (via PayPal), then unfriend you, Kumbaya you, doxx and list you, and Have A Nice Day you.

Tell them I said, "Fuck you".

About the Author

Phil Berto is a retiree with a wicked sense of humor and an old typewriter. When he isn't writing his thoughts to share with his fans and the rest of the world, he enjoys fishing, hunting and motorcycle racing, and finding new ways to annoy his lib-ral acquaintances.

Read more at www.philberto.com.

Made in the USA
Columbia, SC
10 April 2021

35965587R00048